This book belongs to

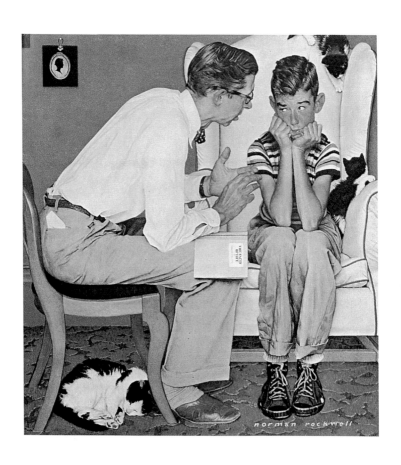

An American Family Album

NORMAN ROCKWELL

ARIEL BOOKS

ANDREWS AND McMEEL

KANSAS CITY

Frontispiece: THE FACTS OF LIFE
Saturday Evening Post cover, July 14, 1951

Book design by Susan Hood

An American Family Album

GRANDPA AT BAT

Saturday Evening Post cover
August 5, 1916

NO SWIMMING

—

Saturday Evening Post cover
June 4, 1921

GRANDPA AND CHILDREN

Literary Digest cover
December 24, 1921

THE ACCOMPANIST

Saturday Evening Post cover
February 3, 1923

DOCTOR AND DOLL

Saturday Evening Post cover
March 9, 1929

HOME FROM VACATION

Saturday Evening Post cover
September 13, 1930

CRAMMING

Saturday Evening Post cover
June 13, 1931

GOING OUT

Saturday Evening Post cover
October 21, 1933

CHILD PSYCHOLOGY

—

Saturday Evening Post cover
November 25, 1933

VACATION

Saturday Evening Post cover
June 30, 1934

THE GIFT

Saturday Evening Post cover
January 25, 1936

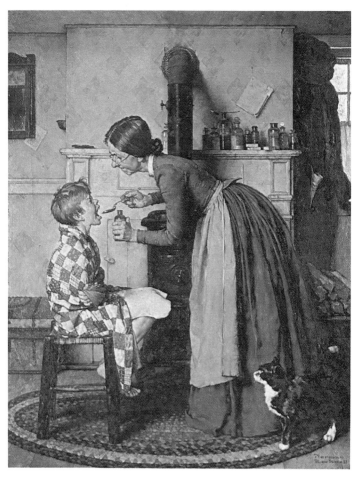

MEDICINE TIME

Saturday Evening Post cover
May 30, 1936

THE NANNY

Saturday Evening Post cover
October 24, 1936

THE COLD

Saturday Evening Post cover
January 23, 1937

DREAMBOATS

Saturday Evening Post cover
February 19, 1938

FIRST FLIGHT

Saturday Evening Post cover
June 4, 1938

AT THE BEACH

Saturday Evening Post cover
July 13, 1940

A SCOUT IS HELPFUL

Boy's Life cover
February, 1942

BACK FROM CAMP

Saturday Evening Post cover
August 24, 1940

FAMILY OUTING

———

Saturday Evening Post cover
August 30, 1947

IT'S GOOD TO BE HOME!

Saturday Evening Post cover
December 25, 1948

PROM DRESS

Saturday Evening Post cover
March 19, 1949

PRACTICE

—

Saturday Evening Post cover
November 18, 1950

FOUR SPORTING BOYS: BASEBALL

Brown & Bigelow
1951 Four Seasons Calendar, Spring

AT THE VET'S

—

Saturday Evening Post cover
March 29, 1952

WALKING TO CHURCH

—

Saturday Evening Post cover
April 4, 1953

GIRL IN THE MIRROR

Saturday Evening Post cover
March 6, 1954

LEAVING HOME

Saturday Evening Post cover
September 25, 1954

THE LOST TOOTH
———

Saturday Evening Post cover
September 7, 1957

THE RUNAWAY

Saturday Evening Post cover
September 20, 1958

THE GRADUATE

Saturday Evening Post cover
June 6, 1959

GUESTS ARRIVING AT A PARTY

—

Saturday Evening Post cover
August 7, 1920

FAMILY GRACE

Ladies' Home Journal
August, 1938